Community Helpers

Farmers

by Cari Meister

Bullfrog Books

Ideas for Parents and Teachers

Bullfrog Books let children practice reading informational text at the earliest reading levels. Repetition, familiar words, and photo labels support early readers.

Before Reading

- Discuss the cover photo. What does it tell them?

- Look at the picture glossary together. Read and discuss the words.

Read the Book

- "Walk" through the book and look at the photos. Let the child ask questions. Point out the photo labels.

- Read the book to the child, or have him or her read independently.

After Reading

- Prompt the child to think more. Ask: Have you ever been to a farm? What kinds of animals lived there? What kinds of plants were growing?

Bullfrog Books are published by Jump!
5357 Penn Avenue South
Minneapolis, MN 55419
www.jumplibrary.com

Library of Congress Cataloging-in-Publication Data
Meister, Cari, author.
  Farmers / by Cari Meister.
    pages cm. — (Community helpers)
  Summary: "This photo-illustrated book for early readers explains what farmers do and how they work to raise crops and animals" — Provided by publisher.
  Audience: 5-8.
  Audience: K to grade 3.
  Includes index.
  ISBN 978-1-62031-092-2 (hardcover)
  ISBN 978-1-62496-160-1 (ebook)
  ISBN 978-1-62031-136-3 (paperback)
  1. Farmers — Juvenile literature.
  2. Farm life — Juvenile literature. I. Title.
  S519.M45 2015
  630 — dc23
                            2013042371

Editor: Wendy Dieker.
Series Designer: Ellen Huber
Book Designer: Lindaanne Donohoe
Photo Researcher: Kurtis Kinneman

Photo Credits: All photos by Shutterstock except Alamy 16; iStock cover

Printed in the United States of America at Corporate Graphics, North Mankato, Minnesota.
6-2014
10 9 8 7 6 5 4 3 2 1

Table of Contents

Farmers at Work

Joe wants to be a farmer.

What do they do?

They grow food.

They take care of animals.

It is spring.

Ty uses a plow.

It breaks up
the dirt.

Now he can
plant crops.

He has a seed drill.

It shoots seeds into the dirt.

He plants corn.

seed

It is fall.

Bo drives a combine.

It harvests wheat.

Wheat can be made
into cereal.

Ken is a dairy farmer.

Moo! He milks cows.

He uses a milker.

milker

Mel is a pig farmer.

Oink! Her sow had babies.

Mel cares for them as
they grow.

Later she sells them.

They will be used
for ham.

Yum!

Farmers grow good food!

On the Farm

barn
Animals stay safe and warm in this building.

silo
A tower where animal feed is stored.

field
Farmers plant crops in fields near their farms.

Picture Glossary

combine
A machine used to harvest grain in the field.

plow
A machine that hooks onto a tractor and is used for turning over soil for planting.

crops
Plants that are grown for food.

seed drill
A machine that hooks onto a tractor and is used for planting seeds in fields.

milker
A machine used to get milk from a cow.

sow
A female pig.

Index

To Learn More

Learning more is as easy as 1, 2, 3.

1) Go to www.factsurfer.com

2) Enter "farmers" into the search box.

3) Click the "Surf" button to see a list of websites.

With factsurfer.com, finding more information is just a click away.